CELEBRATING LIFE

Jewish Rites of Passage

CELEBRATING LIFE
Jewish rites of passage

by Malka Drucker

HOLIDAY HOUSE · NEW YORK

Copyright © 1984 by Malka Drucker
All rights reserved
Printed in the United States of America
First Edition

Library of Congress Cataloging in Publication Data

Drucker, Malka.
  Celebrating life.

  Bibliography: p.
  Includes index.
  Summary: Describes the traditional Jewish ceremonies
celebrating birth, puberty, marriage, and death.
  1. Judaism—Customs and practices—Juvenile literature.
[1. Jews—Rites and ceremonies]   I. Title.   II. Title:
Jewish rites of passage.
BM700.D78 1984   296.4′4   84-4684
ISBN 0-8234-0539-7

For Pam, sister and friend

ACKNOWLEDGMENTS

The author would like to thank Rabbi Harold M. Schulweis and Rabbi Chaim Seidler-Feller for helping with the manuscript. She would also like to thank the Sinai Temple Library's staff for its generosity and patience.

CONTENTS

TO THE READER

When I was a child I sometimes thought that my life was standing still. Even though I understood that I was growing up, I couldn't see it or feel it. I always looked the same to me. What helped me to feel time was passing were my birthdays. Each new candle on the cake helped me to feel more grown-up.

Rites of passage also mark time in a person's life, but they reflect big events: birth, puberty, marriage, and death. This book is about how the Jewish people celebrate and give meaning to these moments. Even though going from one stage of life to the next is natural, it can be frightening—you don't know what to expect. It's exciting but it feels risky. A special ceremony attended by friends and family offers reassurance that the new stage will be O.K.

A rite of passage is not only a private experience, but one that touches the whole Jewish community. The

Bar/Bat Mitzvah ceremony, for example, marks the beginning of moving from childhood to adolescence. This
can be a lonely, anxious, time. The ceremony celebrates
the passage by welcoming the young person as a full
participant in Jewish life.

Celebrating life's turning points helps people to feel
that the stages of life are part of a cycle. Two thousand
years ago, the rabbis suggested this life pattern:

> at 5 one is ready to study Torah (law or
>   teachings)
> at 10 one is ready to study Mishneh
>   (commentaries on the law)
> at 13 one is ready to observe the mitzvot
>   (commandments)
> at 15 one is ready to study Talmud (writings
>   about the Torah)
> at 18 one is ready for marriage
> at 20 one is ready to earn a living
> at 30 one is at the peak of strength
> at 40 one is ready for wisdom
> at 50 one is ready to give counsel
> at 60 old age creeps in
> at 70 there is fullness of years
> at 80 this is an age of strength
> at 90 the body is bent
> and at 100, one is as good as dead.

Because Jewish history spans 4000 years, many ceremonies have their roots in ancient times. At first some of
the customs may seem strange, even out of place in the
modern world. But look at them again. They were

created out of the same wishes, worries, and hopes that people still have, and they still express deep unspoken feelings.

CELEBRATING LIFE
LIFE
Jewish Rites of Passage

I

A CIME CO BE BORN

*And a baby is God's opinion that life
should go on.*

CARL SANDBURG

The most important event in Jewish life is the birth of a
child. Jews bless God every day with their prayers and
God blesses them with children. The first commandment
in the Torah, the five books of the Moses, is to have children: "God said to them, 'Be fertile and fill the earth and
master it.' " (Genesis 1:28) A baby is joyfully welcomed
not only by its parents but by the entire Jewish community.

According to the Talmud, every baby has three parents: the mother, the father, and God. The tradition ex-
plains that the father contributes the white part: bones,
sinews, nails, brain, and the whites of the eyes. The
mother gives the color: skin, flesh, hair, and the darks of

3

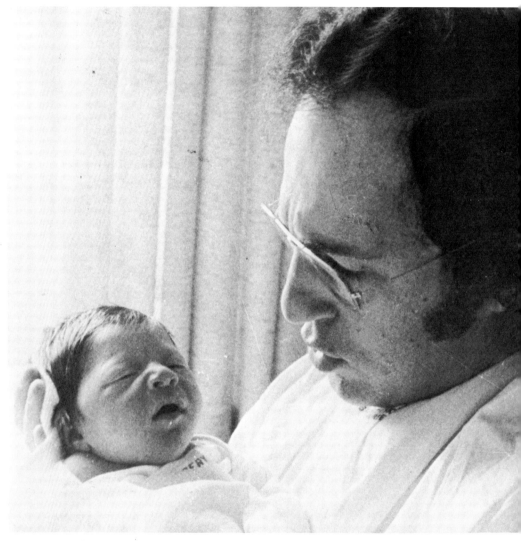

A one-day-old baby with his father.

the eyes. And God gives the baby its spirit, breath, beauty of features, eyesight, hearing, ability to speak and walk, and understanding. Because God is a parent to every child, the mother and father are guardians of the child: he or she is not property but a person with human rights.

Perhaps because no one can remember them, being in the womb and being born are great mysteries. The rabbis said that every baby in its mother's womb has a light burning over its head. At this time the baby can see more of the world than at any time of its life on Earth. Two angels put this light over the baby's head. Meanwhile, another angel finds a soul, which is eternal, and matches it to the baby.

The rabbis also explain how the baby knows so much. Even though a person's body dies, the soul or spirit of that person returns to heaven. This soul or spirit is what made that person unique. The souls live happily in heaven, talking to God and the angels. Then one day God tells one of the souls that it's time to live on Earth for a while. The soul objects, because heaven is so much better than the worries, pain, and problems of Earth. But a commandment is a commandment, so the soul descends into the body of a baby.

While the soul, now part of the baby, is resting in the womb, a respite for what awaits it, an angel comes to visit and takes the baby for a little trip. First the angel takes the baby through its whole life—the baby sees everything that will happen. Then the angel takes the baby to heaven, which is full of sunshine, plenty of food, and people studying happily together. Finally, the angel takes the baby to Gehenna, or hell. It is gloomy, and no one has time to study because everyone is too busy arguing. The angel tells the baby that if it leads a life of goodness and kindness it will end up in heaven. The baby has a lot to think about until birth. At the moment the baby feels the Earth's air, the angel returns, touches the baby on the center of its upper lip—that's why everyone has an indentation there—and the baby forgets its journey as well as its wisdom.

Being pregnant is usually a happy and hopeful time, but it's natural to wonder whether the childbirth will be easy and whether the baby will be normal. Many women try not to talk about these fears. They feel foolish expressing them since the odds are overwhelmingly in favor of a normal birth and a normal child.

In ancient times, though, there was no shame in feeling nervous before childbirth. In fact, a woman would have been considered strange if she didn't worry. The Jewish community supported and helped her from the beginning of her labor. First, a midwife was called as soon as the labor began. The midwife, called a chaya, which means one who brings life, was not alone. Women from the community came to stay and help the woman about to give birth. Not everyone, however, knew she was in labor. There was a superstition that the more people who knew, the harder the labor. This continues among Orthodox Jews today, who don't tell anyone about the pregnancy until it is impossible to conceal.

The women attending the woman in labor helped to ease the labor by opening all the doors, drawers, and chests in the house. They also undid all knots, ties, and buttons. They placed the key of the synagogue in the woman's hand and sometimes a Torah pointer as well.

All these things were supposed to encourage the womb to open easily. Someone usually read the first book of Samuel, too, because it tells of Hannah's joy in having Samuel after years of barrenness.

As soon as the baby was born, even before it was washed, the women each took turns hugging and kissing the baby. Then the chaya sprinkled salt on the baby to protect it from evil spirits and washed it in warm water. She annointed the baby with warm olive oil and powdered it with powder made from ground-up myrtle leaves. After this, the chaya swaddled the baby, which means to wrap the baby tightly in a blanket. If the baby was born in a place where mosquitoes were a problem, the chaya put mashed unripe grapes on the baby's head. This primitive childbirth was less sanitary than modern methods, but it was warm and welcoming for both the mother and her baby.

In Eastern Europe 150 years ago, a baby was always washed in an old tub, one in which children who grew up healthy were bathed. After the bath, the father was called into the room. He threw coins into the tub, which were later given to the midwife. Because Eastern European Jews believed that it was bad luck to prepare for a baby in advance, the baby was always dressed in old clothes. Some Jews still observe this superstition and do not buy anything for the baby until it is born.

As soon as the baby was born, the parents thanked God by saying the Shehecheyanu: "You abound in blessings, Lord our God, Ruler of the Universe, Who has granted us life and sustained us and brought us to this moment." This prayer, which is said whenever anything new and special happens, is still said at childbirth.

The parents of a baby also planted a cedar tree for a boy and a pine tree for a girl in honor of the birth. The trees would be cut to make the bridal canopy of the child at the time of his or her marriage. Everyone hoped the child would grow and thrive like a tree. Many Jewish parents today, no matter where they live, plant a tree in Israel (this is done for them by the Jewish National Fund) as part of this tradition of tree planting at birth.

The baby's cradle is also very special. European Jews often used a large bread trough into which they threw sugar, raisins, cake, and coins before the baby was put in it. Although modern parents don't use a bread trough anymore, some still throw sweets into the cradle as a wish for the baby's life to be sweet.

From the moment a baby boy was born until his circumcision eight days later, or a girl until she was twenty days old, the mother and baby were surrounded by amulets, which are charms, to ward off Lilith, the evil spirit who stole babies. There are very few Jews who still use these amulets, much to modern rabbis' relief. No matter how much the rabbis disapproved of this protection, people insisted on the custom. Bells were put on the cradle, a circle drawn with chalk or flour would enclose the room. The circle was supposed to keep Lilith outside it. The Sh'ma, the most important Jewish prayer, was said every night. Candles were also lit to protect the mother and the baby.

Lilith is the mystery woman of the Torah. According to the Talmud, she was the first woman, not Eve. The Torah says that man and woman were created at the same time: "And God created the human species in His

One of the forests in Israel planted by Jews from all over the world.
Sometimes trees are planted for a special occasion, such as a
birth or a Bar/Bat Mitzvah. The sign says: NATURE PRESERVE.

JEWISH NATIONAL FUND

own image . . . male and female created He them."
(Genesis 1:27) Adam was the male and Lilith was the female. Adam began to tell Lilith to do things for him, and
she refused because he didn't consider her his equal.
Adam complained to God, Lilith complained to God,
and God did nothing. Finally, Lilith couldn't stand
being with Adam anymore, so she left Eden. Adam
asked God to find her and bring her back, so He sent
three angels and told them, "Explain to her that if she
doesn't come back 100 of her children will die daily."
The angels found her on the bottom of the ocean and de-
livered the message. Lilith chose to stay, and the legend
goes on to tell how she steals newborn babies as revenge
for the loss of her children. Without Lilith, Adam was
lonely, so God created Eve to keep him company.

In ancient times, the night before a newborn boy's
circumcision was a time to carefully watch and protect
the mother and child from Lilith. The evening eventually became a happy time of food, prayer, and Torah
readings. The watch night is no longer observed, but
some Jews have a party on the first Friday evening after
a baby is born. The custom, called Shalom Zachar,
which means greeting the male, includes friends and relatives who wish to share the family's joy in the great
event. Families have also begun to include girls with a
Shalom Nekavah (greeting the female) celebration. At
both these ceremonies parts of the Torah and psalms
(songs of praise) are read.

Everyone eats cake and fruit, and drinks sweet wine.
Lentils and garbanzo beans are often part of the meal
because their roundness represents the life cycle. They
are also served at the meal that follows a funeral. Some

This 18th Century Italian silver amulet was supposed to protect a newborn baby and its mother from Adam's first wife, Lilith.

say that the likeness of food at both occasions is because the mother, delighted as she is with her new baby, bears some sadness—the child is no longer part of her and has forgotten all that he or she knew in her womb.

2

WELCOME!

*To everything there is a season, and a time
to every purpose under heaven . . .*

ECCLESIASTES

Of all the customs surrounding a birth, one of the most
important is naming the baby. Friends and family may
be curious about what names the parents have chosen,
but if the family is traditional they won't ask. They will
wait for the suspense to be broken at the baby's public
naming. A boy's name will be announced eight days
after birth, at his Brit Milah (covenant of circumcision).
A girl will be named in a synagogue on the first Shabbat
after her birth or at a special ceremony at home called
either a Simhat Habat (celebration of the daughter), Brit
Hayim (covenant of life), or at a Brit Bat (covenant of
the daughter).

Jewish children often have four names, two in English

or whatever the native language of the country in which they are born, and two in Hebrew. For example, a baby's name might be Molly Susan in English and Malka Shulamith in Hebrew. The first initials usually are the same. Some families give their child an American name that is also a Hebrew name, such as David or Deborah. Whatever the parents decide, they probably consider more than its pretty sound when they search for an appropriate name.

The Jewish tradition takes names seriously. God's name is so important that He told it only to Moses. God, Jehovah, Lord, Adonai, Elohim, are only substitutes for the real name. In ancient times children were often named after plants or animals, either because their parents loved the natural world or because they wanted the child to have the characteristics of the plant or animal. A name could also be connected to a parent. Isaac means laughter, because when Sarah, an old woman who had long given up her dream of having a child, was told by God that she and Abraham would have a child, she laughed, but not purely from joy. She simply thought it ridiculously funny that someone as old as Abraham could sire a child.

In the Torah, people's names change as they grow and change. When God spoke to Abraham and told him that he would be the father of a great nation, God changed his name from Abram to Abraham and Sarai's name to Sarah. Abraham meant God notices, and Sarah meant princess. All Hebrew names have meaning. The most dramatic name change in the Torah happened to Jacob, Isaac and Rebecca's son. Jacob had stolen the privileges entitled to his twin brother, Esau, by deceiving Isaac.

Jacob made his arm hairy like Esau's by covering it with animal fur. Putting his blind father's hand on his arm he said, "Father, I am Easu. Give me my birthright."

Jacob worried constantly about what Esau might do to him, and he finally decided to apologize and give him many goats, cows, camels, bulls, and sheep. He sent a messenger to Esau telling him of his plan.

Still he worried that Esau would kill him when they met. The night before the meeting Jacob talked to God and told him how scared he was and how much he hoped God would save him. He also reminded God that He promised to make Jacob a father of the Jewish people. Then he went off to sleep alone, away from his wives and children. He awakened to find someone who looked like a man wrestling with him. Jacob wrestled hard and was beating the man-angel who tried to escape him. But Jacob wouldn't let him go until the angel blessed him. The angel said, "Your name is no longer Jacob, but Israel." Israel means one who has striven with God and has won.

After his naming he went out to greet his brother, Esau, with courage. Esau embraced him and they both wept. Jacob grew up by facing his fear. Only then could he be a leader of the Jewish people. When a parent names a child Jacob (Yaakov in Hebrew), he or she hopes that the child will have the courage the first Jacob possessed when he corrected the wrong he committed against his warrior brother.

The Torah also tries to remind a parent that a bad name can be as destructive as a good name can help a child to be strong. When Jacob's wife, Rachel, lay dying from having given birth, she named the baby Ben-oni, which means son of my suffering. Jacob, who understood the power of a name, renamed the boy Ben-jamin, the son of the right hand.

Two thousand years ago Jews began to name their children not only after great figures in the Bible, but after dead relatives whom they wished to honor. The Jews probably borrowed this custom from the Egyptians and Greeks, who named their children after dead grand-parents. Ashkenazic Jews, who are Jews descended from Eastern European families, still follow this custom. Often only the first letter of a name is used. A baby named for his great-grandfather Morris might be named Max and his Hebrew name could be Moshe. His middle name can honor another dead relative. Sephardic Jews, whose families originally lived in Spain and the Middle East, name their children after living relatives, but rarely after a parent. There are very few Jewish "Jun-iors." There are no laws about children's names, only customs, but most parents follow them. So, if someone wanted to name her child Ripe Raisin, Jewish law would have no objection.

The Brit Milah is an ancient ceremony that is de-scribed in Genesis, the first book of the Torah, as some-thing every Jewish parent must do on the eighth day after a boy's birth. The father, or sometimes the mother, must provide for the removal of the foreskin from the baby's penis. This is called circumcision, and it is the outward mark of a Jewish male belonging to the Jewish community.

A Brit is a covenant, which means an agreement or promise and Milah means to cut. So Brit Milah is a pun, because in Hebrew the common expression is to cut a

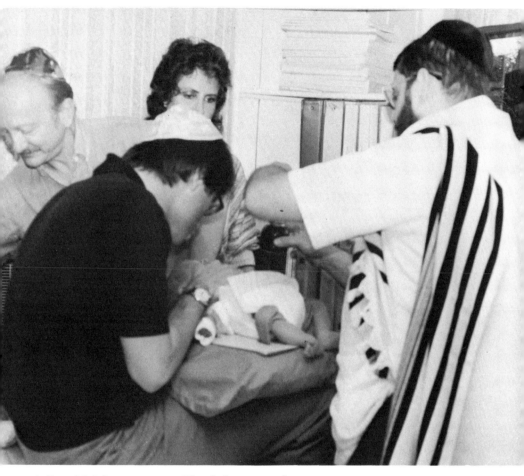

A Brit Milah ceremony. The baby is on the
sandek's lap; the mohel is on right.

DAVID TUCH

covenant rather than to make one. When God showed Noah the rainbow after the flood, that was God's Brit to Noah never to flood the Earth again. The rainbow was a sign of renewal. The Sabbath is another promise. As a holy day that symbolizes the completion of Creation, it holds the promise of how good the world will be in the world to come. The Brit Milah is God's promise that the Jewish people will continue to exist. That is why the ceremony centers around the body part which helps to create future generations.

The first Brit Milah mentioned in the Torah was Abraham's. The most dramatic description of a Brit Milah occurs later in the Torah where it is written that Moses became very sick in the wilderness and was about to die. His wife, Zipporah, and son, Gershom, were with him. Zipporah, convinced that the illness was punishment for Moses having failed to circumcise Gershom, had to act fast. "So Zipporah took a flint and cut off her son's foreskin, saying, 'You are truly a bridegroom of blood to me!' And when He let him [Moses] alone, she added, 'A bridegroom of blood because of the circumcision.' " (Ex. 4:24–26)

Jews did not invent circumcision and they are not the only people to practice it. In fact, most boys in the United States are circumcised today for health reasons. It is also done as a puberty rite by tribes in Africa, Asia, the South Pacific, and among some Native American tribes. It was also done by the ancient Egyptians, Phoenicians, and Arabs. The Jewish people borrowed this custom but changed it from being a puberty rite to a birth rite. By changing the time for this rite of passage, the Jews changed its meaning, too. It became a religious

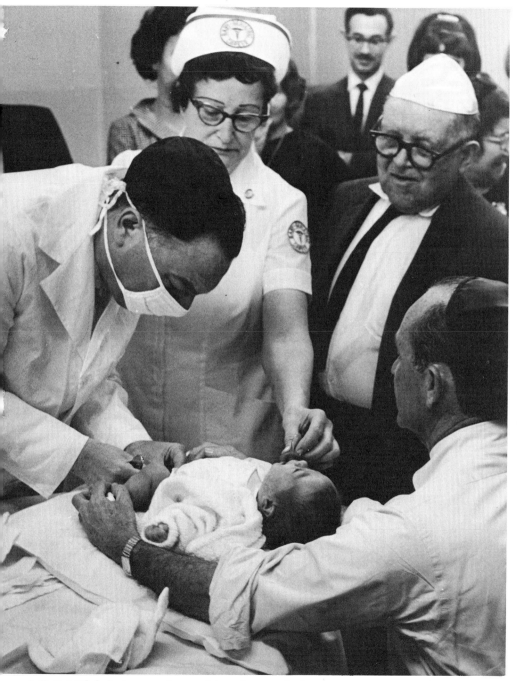

A Brit Milah being performed in a hospital. A nurse
assists the mohel who is wearing a face mask.

IRVING HERZBERG

rite that expressed the covenant between God and the Jewish people.

The Torah does not explain why the Brit Milah must take place on the eighth day (unless the baby isn't strong enough and then it's postponed), but it is thought that some rabbis believed every baby must experience seven days of Creation so that he contains the whole world within him before the Brit. It also means that the baby will know the sweetness of the Sabbath. Another idea is that seven days represent the whole world and the eighth day represents the world to come.

In Biblical times, the baby's father circumcised his son with a sharp knife or a flint. But for at least two thousand years, a mohel, who is especially trained in the prayers and procedure, has performed the Brit Milah for a family. It is a ceremony of great drama, and like all rites of passage, it has special meaning for the Jewish people as well as for the child.

Sephardic Jews have the Brit in a synagogue, as it was done in ancient times, but Ashkenazic Jews have the ceremony at home. Since most American Jews are Ashkenazic, most Brits take place at home. Usually they are in the morning to show that it is a mitzvah, a positive commandment, that everyone is eager to do. The mohel wears a white robe and kippah (head covering) that looks religious and surgical at the same time. While he sets up his instruments, the baby is bathed by his mother with the help of her friends.

When the mohel is ready, the kvatterin, a woman given the honor of bringing in the baby, enters with him. The mohel says loudly, "Baruh Haba!" ("Blessed be he who comes," or simply "Welcome"). Everyone in the room may say this, too. This is usually the first time friends and family have seen the little boy, and it's their chance to greet him. Everyone stands up during the ceremony. No one knows how much this eight day old baby understands, but he may enjoy having a roomful of people with welcoming smiles.

Some people light candles in the room and place a special chair near where the ceremony will be. In Eastern Europe this chair, called Elijah's chair, often was a double chair. The sandek, or godfather, sat on one side, Elijah on the other. Being a sandek is the greatest honor at a Brit, and it is usually given to one of the baby's grandfathers. Elijah was a prophet who, according to Jewish tradition, will announce the coming of the Messiah. Because the Messiah could be any Jewish child, he has to be at every Brit so that he doesn't miss the baby who will grow up to lead the world to justice, mercy, peace, and plenty.

Most people do not have a fancy double chair, so they take a special chair called a kiseh shel eliahu, which means the chair of Elijah. The baby rests on a pillow which can be an ordinary bed pillow or something very fancy that has been decorated especially for his big day. After the prayers, the parents may want to tell everyone how they came to choose the baby's names, which will be formally announced after the circumcision. They may talk about what kind of people the baby is being named for. If the parents are not actually circumcising their son, they hand the mohel the knife. This is a way of saying, "This is my job, and I'm asking you to represent me."

Then the mohel gives the baby to the sandek and says,

This ornate Kiseh shel Eliahu, Elijah's chair,
was used in Germany during the 19th Century.

"Praised are You, O Lord our God, King of the Universe, Who has sanctified us with Your commandments, and commanded us concerning the rite of circumcision." The procedure, which takes just a minute or two, is performed with modern surgicial instruments. There is usually no more than a drop or two of blood. The sandek is supposed to hold the baby and pillow on his knees, but most mohels prefer to work on a steady waist-high table, so the sandek simply stands beside the mohel and holds the baby still.

Immediately after the circumcision the father, and sometimes the mother, too, says, "You abound in blessings, Lord our God, Ruler of the Universe, Who has sanctified us with Your commandments and has commanded us to bring him (the child) into the Covenant of our father, Abraham." Relieved the circumcision is over, everyone says "Amen," and, "Just as he entered the covenant, so may he enter into a study of Torah, into marriage, and into doing good deeds."

While these lofty goals are being said, the mohel diapers the person who, one hopes, eventually will do these mitzvot. The mohel gives the baby to his father, says the blessings over wine, and announces: Let his name be called in Israel _____, the son of _____ and _____. The baby gets a few drops of wine rubbed on his lips so that he can participate in his first ceremony as a new member welcomed into the covenant. The wine often stops the baby's crying, but if the mohel gives him a piece of gauze wetted in a mixture of sugar and a little wine before the ceremony, he may not be crying at all but nearly asleep. If he's not too sleepy, his mother will nurse him or give him a bottle and put him to sleep.

In Eastern Europe, a baby would have some strange objects in his cradle before he fell asleep. There would be a small Torah so that he might fulfill what is written in it, and a quill and ink bottle as an omen that he might grow up to be worthy of being a scribe or writer of the Torah. In fact, the diaper used during the Brit Milah may be made—after it's washed—into a wimpel, a piece of cloth that keeps the spools of the Torah together.

The Brit ends with a Seudat Mitzvah, a feast which follows the ceremony. The meal is a pleasant way to end the ceremony, but that's not the only reason for it. The Talmud says it is a commandment just as much as the circumcision itself. The tradition may have begun with Abraham and Sarah, who gave a "great feast on the day that Isaac was weaned." All Jewish celebrations, whether they are part of a holiday or a rite of passage, include a special meal. Maybe that's why when Jews think back to a memorable event such as a Bar Mitzvah or a Sabbath, they often remember how soft and fragrant the hallah (festival bread) was, or how delicious the chocolate dessert was.

The Brit Milah allows very little time for preparation, so the meal is usually cold food. Herring is almost always present, because it is a sign of fertility, and there is sweet food for the baby's future. Whatever the food, the meal is joyful, because a new baby is a wonderful reason for Jews to celebrate. They have a new member of the family, and he belongs to all of them.

When the baby is a month old, if he is the firstborn

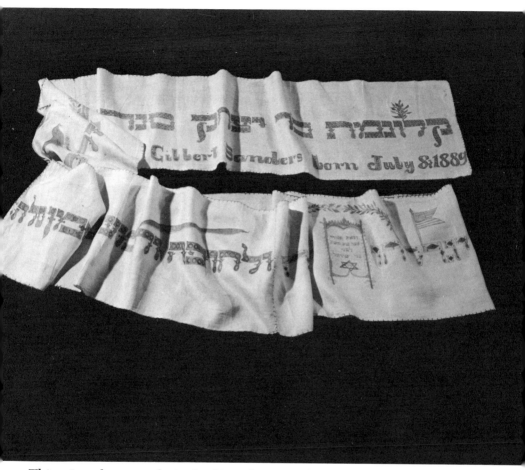

This wimpel was made in the United States almost 100 years
ago. It has American and Jewish symbols decorating it.

child, his family has a Pidyon Haben, a ceremony almost as ancient as the Brit Milah. It means "redemption of the firstborn [male]." There are three families, or tribes, of Jews: the Kohanim are the priests; the Levites are the priests' helpers; and the Israelites are the rest of the people. God told Moses to take every first firstborn and make him responsible for taking care of the great Temple. But when the Jewish people melted their gold and turned it into a golden calf to worship, the only tribe that didn't worship the calf was the Levites. However, because the firstborn were once chosen by God, they had to be freed from Temple service. This was done by the child's father giving a Kohen five silver shekels. Even though the Temple no longer exists, the ceremony still is done.

For many people the meaning of the Pidyon Haben is simple: it is a ceremony which acknowledges the special feeling a parent has for a firstborn child. This doesn't mean that parents will love this child more than their other children, but the experience of being a parent for the first time is wondrous, and the firstborn child is part of that experience.

The ceremony is brief. The Kohen, who is anyone descended from the priestly tribe of the Kohenim, is the leader. Jews with names like Cohen or Kaplan are usually Kohanim as well as other Jews whose names give no clue. He doesn't have to be a rabbi. The Kohen asks the father if he wants to give him his son or redeem him for five shekels, which are in the form of silver dollars or special Pidyon Haben coins the Israeli government has minted. The father replies that he would like to redeem his son. Then the Kohen takes the money, holds it over the little boy's head, and says, "This money is in place of that . . . May this child enter into life, into the Torah and a fear of heaven." The Kohen puts the money aside, blesses the baby, says another blessing over wine, and then the ceremony ends. Once again there is a Seudat Mitzvah, one that the parents can enjoy a little more than the Brit Milah, because they are now more accustomed to their child. The Kohen usually returns the money when the ceremony is over, and the parents often give the money to charity.

The Brit Milah and Pidyon Haben are ceremonies for boys. What about girls? The Jewish tradition recognizes that women, as well as men, are made in God's image, but it has favored men. When a son was born in ancient times, it was a time for rejoicing, because he could support himself and his family in their old age. A daughter meant providing a dowry, a gift to her husband. So having sons was better than daughters from that society's point of view.

But since Jews no longer live in the ancient world, many of them are no longer comfortable with so many lovely ceremonies that welcome boys but exclude girls. So new and exciting rituals have been created to include girls into the covenant. Because they love and respect the tradition, those Jews who are creating new ceremonies structure them like the Brit Milah and Pidyon Haben.

Baby girls were traditionally named in the synagogue within the first month of their birth. The mother sometimes came along. The father went up to the Torah to say the blessings over it and also said the Mi Sheberah: "May the God Who blessed our fathers Abraham, Isaac,

and Jacob, Moses and Aaron, David and Solomon, may
He bless the mother _____ and her newborn
daughter, whose name in Israel shall be called
_____. May they raise her for the marriage
canopy and for a life of good deeds." Both boys and girls
have these blessings in synagogues today, even if they've
been named at home before. It's a way for the entire
congregation to participate in the simha, or joy of the
event.

The new naming ceremonies, Brit Hayim, Brit Bat,
and Simhat Habat are celebrated at home within a week
to two weeks after a baby girl's birth. The three ceremonies closely follow the order of the Brit Milah, except, of
course, there is no circumcision. The baby girl is carried
in. Everyone wishes her "Baruha Haba'ah!," and then
her mother and father say the blessings together and
name her. Some people follow the words of the Brit
Milah, while others use the Mi Sheberah with this
change: "May her mother and father merit to see her
joyously celebrating under the wedding canopy, de-
lighting in the study of Torah, and dedicating herself to
a life of moral behavior. May they further see her a radi-
ant mother of children and grandchildren, prosperous
and well respected, vigorous and flourishing, filled with
sap and freshness into a productive old age. May this be
your will and let us say Amen."

The wish for her to study Torah is new. Traditionally
that was only for boys. The ceremony ends with a Seudat Mitzvah. These ceremonies are so new nearly everyone is different, but that also makes them more personal
and fresh.

Maybe it's because Jews are a small part of the

A father and mother at their daughter's Brit Bat. The baby rests on a pillow made especially for the ceremony.

world's population and they worry about disappearing, or maybe it's God's first commandment, "Be fruitful and multiply," or maybe some may believe that the 21-inch person in diapers is the Messiah, but whatever the reason, these ceremonies which celebrate a Jewish child's birth are a strong sweet memory for those who go to them. Even though it can be embarassing when some distant uncle comes up, pinches someone on the cheek, and says, "I was at your Bris" (Yiddish for Brit), one tries to be understanding. The uncle feels close to the person because he witnessed a major rite of passage in his or her life.

3
GROWING UP

The father must rebuke his child to improve his behavior, but he should do so pleasantly and not cruelly, and he is forbidden to hit his older son.

TALMUD

Birth is a time for great rejoicing, but it's the child's physical, intellectual, and spiritual growth that quickly captures the family's attention. Maybe that's why the weaning ceremony was more important in ancient times than the Brit Milah. Weaning was a sign of a child's growing up.

It's a mitzvah (commandment) for parents to teach their child Torah, which is not only the five books of Moses. The rabbis believed that learning Torah is a form of prayer which can guide a child into being a caring, generous person.

For two thousand years parents have fulfilled the mitzvah of teaching Torah to their children by sending them to school. All children, even if they were poor or orphans, were educated. They went to school every day, often in the evening, and on holidays, too. In Eastern Europe little boys (girls were taught at home by their mothers) began school at five. The first day of school was special, a little rite of passage. The father gathered up his little boy in his prayer shawl and carried him to school in it. The teacher wrote letters on a blackboard, but he didn't use chalk. He used honey. When the little boy could say the letter, the teacher took the child's finger and traced the letter. The boy, who sucked his sticky finger, was supposed to think of learning as a sweet experience.

The teacher in Jewish life was highly respected. The Talmud asks, "If you had two errands to run, one for your father and one for your teacher, whose errand would you do first?" The answer is, your teacher, because of what he has given you. A child's education was not only a mitzvah but the parents' gift as well. At times the Jewish people have lived under dangerous and difficult circumstances. When they lived in countries that didn't want them, they often weren't allowed to own land or a business. They were poor, but they held onto their dignity by being a learned people. No one could take their ideas, and nothing could stop them from knowing as much as kings.

The most important rite of passage while growing up is the Bar/Bat Mitzvah at thirteen. This ceremony of adolescence is probably the best-known Jewish ritual, but it is also the most misunderstood. A person becomes a

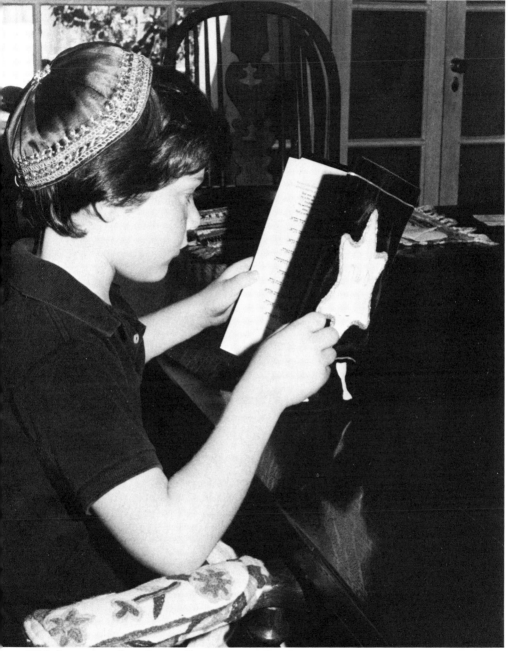

This boy is reading his Hebrew prayer book. Many Jewish children begin to learn Hebrew when they are six.

STEPHANIE SABAR

Bar/Bat Mitzvah when he or she reaches thirteen. It is also the name for the ceremony that celebrates becoming thirteen. It doesn't celebrate how much you've learned or how much you've accomplished up to this point in your life. What it does celebrate is the shift from childhood to adulthood. During this fragile time, there are physical changes. But there is also an inner transformation of an awakening spirit that wants to repair the world. It is this idealism that the Bar/Bat Mitzvah ceremony celebrates.

Entering the teenage years is a serious step in Jewish life. The tradition expects the Bar/Bat Mitzvah to keep Jewish laws expected of an adult and be responsible for one's conduct. He or she is allowed to read from the Torah and be part of a minyan, which is a group of at least ten people necessary to say certain daily prayers.

Parents of a Bar/Bat Mitzvah are no longer responsible for their child's decisions. Some parents say this prayer at the Bar/Bat Mitzvah: "Blessed is He Who has freed me from responsibility for this child's conduct." This doesn't mean that the parents no longer care about their children now that they are thirteen, but they recognize that it's time to give them room to develop their characters. Now it's up to them to care about other people and have a sense of social responsibility. The parents can't force any of them to become a mensch, which is Yiddish for being a generous, honorable, and compassionate person.

The Talmud says that the evil impulse is thirteen years older than the good impulse. The evil impulse begins when a child is in the womb and continues to develop when he is born. The child doesn't have anything our son, ivan matthew

יצחק עמשה

will be called to the torah
as a bar mitzvah
saturday, the nineteenth of march
nineteen hundred and eighty-three
at eight forty-five in the morning

we would be delighted
to have you share our joy

please join us
for kiddush and luncheon
following the services
at valley beth shalom
15739 ventura boulevard
encino, california

malka and steven drucker

An invitation to a Bar Mitzvah ceremony.

inside him to stop him from doing the wrong thing. At thirteen the good impulse is born. If the child breaks the Sabbath or hurts someone, something inside him senses the wrongdoing. The Talmud also says that a Bar Mitzvah gets an extra soul because he becomes more closely connected to God through doing good deeds. A baby is born with the makings of this soul, but it doesn't come together until age thirteen.

Why thirteen? There is no single answer. The Torah does not mention anything about a Bar Mitzvah, but there are clues. It may be because Abraham rejected his father's idolatry when he was thirteen. Supposedly Jacob and Esau went their separate ways at thirteen. The Talmud says that a thirteen-year-old's promise counts as much as an adult's. In ancient times thirteen was the age of marriage. By the first century, a thirteen-year-old was able to participate in all religious rituals.

Becoming a Bar Mitzvah became a ceremony during the Middle Ages. The Bat Mitzvah ceremony began in the 1920's, when the Conservative and Reform movements decided that girls should have the same welcome as boys for reaching the age of full religious participation.

Until shortly before World War II, becoming a Bar Mitzvah was a quiet rite of passage which required little planning and preparation. When a boy reached thirteen, he went to the synagogue with his father on Monday, Thursday, Saturday, or Rosh Hodesh (the holiday that celebrates the new moon). These are the days when the Torah is read, and he went on the day closest to his thirteenth birthday. During the service he was called to the Torah to be given the honor of chanting an aliyah, the prayers said before and after the reading of the Torah. He might also have been given part of the Torah to read. This ceremony recognized him as an adult Jew.

After the service, the men of the congregation (unless it was Shabbat, women probably wouldn't be there) congratulated him upon becoming a Bar Mitzvah. Then he and his father went home for a special meal, the Seudat Mitzvah, that his mother would have prepared in honor of the occasion.

The Bar/Bat Mitzvah has become a prominent Jewish ceremony, perhaps because much more studying is necessary today. Until about 100 years ago, the Bar Mitzvah was just another step in a young man's life. He began school young, learned his prayers as soon as he could talk, and certainly could read Hebrew. He needed no special training to become a Bar Mitzvah. Becoming a Bar Mitzvah was no more a major event than being able to vote. It changed his status in the community, but nothing else was given him by becoming a Bar Mitzvah. Like a good soldier, he was simply expected to accept the mitzvot as his instruments for repairing the world.

The Bar/Bat Mitzvah ceremony still confers adult status upon thirteen-year-olds, but it has taken on other meanings as well. For many young people, becoming a Bar/Bat Mitzvah represents years of going to classes after school to learn Hebrew and Torah. Many children begin at five. Most synagogues will not allow a child to become a Bar/Bat Mitzvah unless they have had at least five years of religious schooling.

Because Jews outside Israel live in two worlds, the country they live in and their Jewish world, it takes a special effort for parents to teach their children Torah. The Bar/Bat Mitzvah ceremony celebrates this effort. Until modern times, Jews didn't have the luxury of deciding whether to raise their children as Jews. They knew only one world, and they stuck to it. Even if they wanted to abandon Judaism, the non-Jewish world would not allow it. A child today who becomes a Bar/Bat Mitzvah does it by choice. Perhaps that choice has given the ceremony a new meaning.

Most Bar/Bat Mitzvah ceremonies take place on the Sabbath, because the sweet rest of Shabbat adds something special to becoming a Bar/Bat Mitzvah. There are also many more people at the morning Shabbat service than at any other service of the week. Some families, though, who prefer a small service only attended by friends and family, will have the ceremony during the week. Reform Jews hold Bar/Bat Mitzvah ceremonies on Friday night as well as Saturday morning.

The Bar/Bat Mitzvah says much more than an aliyah at the service. On the bima, the platform, for the entire service, he or she will chant at least part of the Torah portion, and some children, depending upon their skill, will recite the whole reading. The portion becomes an intimate link to the Torah, because the Bar/Bat Mitzvah has come to know it so well. Reading from the Torah publicly is a great honor and a sign of growing up.

The Bar/Bat Mitzvah may also recite the Haftorah, a part of the Prophets. Both of these texts are in Hebrew, but the Torah portion is much more difficult. It has no vowels and the characters are very fancy, almost like reading Gothic script. Most people who read from the Torah use a pointer to keep their place. Both the Torah

This Bar Mitzvah is reading a Haftorah
during the Shabbat morning service.

and Haftorah must be chanted, or sung. The boy or girl says the last word of the blessings. After the Haftorah, the congregation throws lots of candy at him. If he's quick, he'll duck behind the lectern and then scramble to pick some of it up.

The Bar/Bat Mitzvah will also give a drasha, or speech, about the meaning of the Torah or Haftorah. This is to show that the young person can think. That person is now not only a student but a teacher as well. Now he or she is a source of Torah and has entered the community of learned Jews. The Bar/Bat Mitzvah may also get the chance to lead the congregation in some of the prayers. Standing in front of several hundred people while you chant Biblical Hebrew with a person at your side to correct you at the slightest mistake takes courage. As happy as a Bar/Bat Mitzvah may be with the privilege of participation, there is a sense of relief when the service is over, and he or she can enjoy the Seudat Mitzvah, which is often a large lunch or dinner attended by relatives and friends.

Becoming a Bar/Bat Mitzvah allows you to wear a tallit, which is a prayer shawl, and tefillin, which are two little boxes with leather straps. Until this point, the only religious garment a child could wear was a kippah, or head covering. But a Bar/Bat Mitzvah is entitled to wear the full uniform of an adult Jew. Traditionally, the tallit and tefillin are only given to boys, but some Conservative and Reform congregations require the same responsibilities of boys and girls.

The tallit is a large shawl that when worn comes down to one's fingertips. It is rectangular, often has stripes, and always has four fringes. It is worn whenever

A Bat Mitzvah wearing her tallit.

a Jew prays in daylight. It is not worn at night. The fringes represent the four corners of the universe that God has made, and all the knots plus the four fringes add up to 613, which is the number of mitzvot in the Torah. Wearing these fringes is a Biblical commandment.

In ancient times the hem of a person's robe told one how important the person was. The more fringes on the hem, the more powerful the person. God told the Jewish people that they were all important, that they—and not just the rich and learned—were all priests. Everyone, men and women, rich and poor, was commanded to wear fringes. The Torah doesn't say, however, when a person should start wearing a tallit. Traditionally, a man would not wear a tallit until he got married. His bride often gave him one as a wedding present. Some Orthodox Jews still follow this practice, but most families give a tallit at the time of becoming a Bar Mitzvah. The boy holds the tallit in front of him and says the blessing: "You abound in blessings, Lord our God, Ruler of the Universe, Who has sanctified us with His commandments, and commanded us to enwrap ourselves in [a tallit with] fringes." Then he puts it over his shoulders.

The tefillin are also part of a Biblical commandment: "And thou shall bind them for a sign upon thine hand, and they shall be for frontlets between thine eyes." Within each box, which is usually made of leather and covered with wood or silver, are four sections of the Torah which mention tefillin.

A Bar/Bat Mitzvah is supposed to wear the tefillin every day for morning prayers during the week; they are not worn on Shabbat or holidays. One box is worn on the left bicep, facing the heart, and the other box is placed

Tefillin with silver cases for the boxes when the tefillin isn't being worn. The bag is for carrying the tefillin to and from the synagogue.

on the forehead. The straps are wound around the left forearm and hand in a special pattern. The box on the forehead has the letter, Shin, 𝕎 on it, the knot of the strap looks like the letter, Daled, ד and the knot near the box on the arm looks like the letter, Yud ׳ . These three letters spell Shaddai, one of the names for God Almighty.

At first it takes a long time to get it right, without the straps being so tight your fingers turn purple or so loose that the boxes slip. Once you do get it on, the tefillin and tallit may feel strange to wear, but after a while you get

A Bar Mitzvah putting on tefillin.

so used to them you can't imagine praying without them. They become cues to help you concentrate on the prayers and feeling connected to God. The straps bind you, the tallit enfolds you, and together they help to take you from everyday concerns for a while.

An American Jew once visited Spain and became friends with a young man who, like most Spaniards, was Catholic. He invited the American to his house and showed him the family chapel where they held Mass. Off that room was a small room no larger than a closet. It contained only a small wooden bureau. The visitor asked what the room was for. The young man explained that when a family member had a grave problem, he would go into that room, take from the bureau a holy object that had been in the family for generations, and meditate.

He took his friend into the room and opened the bureau. The visitor recognized the object at once—it was tefillin! How this Catholic family came to own and cherish tefillin was a mystery, but it was possible that the family had been Jewish until the Inquisition in the fifteenth century. Many Jews converted publicly but retained their Jewishness at home. This family became Christian but did not want to give up the holy power of tefillin.

In the nineteenth century, German Reform Jews decided that the Bar Mitzvah at thirteen was too young to give a person full adult status in Jewish life. They did away with the Bar Mitzvah and introduced the confirmation at sixteen. Although the Bar/Bat Mitzvah is still practiced in the United States, Conservative and Reform Jews also have confirmation ceremonies. Thirteen-year-olds aren't always interested in the preparations and plans for the Bar/Bat Mitzvah. They may simply do what they are asked by teachers and parents.

But by the time they are sixteen, they may have some ideas about how they feel about their Jewishness. Confirmation class offers a chance to talk about this. Later they may express these feelings at the confirmation ceremony, which usually takes place at the Friday night Shabbat service. If they have doubts about God, about Israeli politics, or about temple politics, they are free to say so. The tradition has always encouraged questions, doubt, and disagreements. Abraham and Moses argued with God, Jacob wrestled with Him, and their connection with God set an example. Some people turn away from the synagogue because they have these feelings. This is a chance to speak with freedom and honesty within the synagogue. Bar/Bat Mitzvah and confirmation aren't farewell ceremonies to the synagogue. Instead, they are rites that allow one to speak up and be part of Jewish life in a new, important way.

4

MARRIAGE

For love is strong as death
Harsh as the grave
Its tongues are flames
A fierce and holy blaze.

SONG OF SONGS

In the Jewish tradition life on Earth is more important than heaven or hell. You can feel the sweetness of the world to come in everyday life. You don't have to die to know paradise. The tradition also teaches that you can feel God's presence while you live, but you need to be with someone else, because God dwells between people. Some traditions teach that the highest spiritual state a person can reach is by separating oneself from earthly possessions and relationships. The highest state for a Jew is to sit beside one's mate and watch one's children and grandchildren harvest the family fields.

Marriage is an essential experience of Jewish life. In ancient times, no one remained unmarried intentionally. A man and woman were not considered whole until they found a mate. The Talmud says: "Until the age of twenty, the Holy One sits and waits. 'When will he take a wife?' But as soon as one attains the age of twenty and is not yet married, He exclaims, 'Blasted be his bones!' " Marriage is one of the three great hopes everyone wishes for when a child is born. The parents hope the child will study Torah, be under the wedding canopy, and do good deeds.

One of the most important reasons to get married is to have children. Children make marriage holy, because marriage is where God's image is reproduced. In ancient times, not to have children, if you were able, was almost as serious as taking someone's life.

Until the twentieth century, love was never a reason to get married. In Eastern Europe, falling in love was considered a disease that needed a speedy cure. Girls rarely left the house except to draw water from the well, so they had little chance of meeting a boy on their own. Fathers always arranged the marriages, sometimes when the bride and groom were still in diapers. The groom was chosen for his father's and uncles' scholarship, or his own if he was old enough. Learning was better than wealth or nobility of blood. If the young man came from a different town than the bride, her family would test him to see the depth of his learning.

The bride was chosen for her family wealth and appearance. Beautiful eyes meant a beautiful woman. Patience was also valued. The women in the groom's family might give her a tangled thread that she had to

19th Century wedding in Germany.

unknot. Sometimes she had to make dough and then cut it into spaghetti-thin strips.

The Talmud says that all matches are made in heaven before a child is born. King Solomon had a beautiful daughter. He scanned the stars and discovered that she would marry the poorest man in Israel. So he locked her in a high tower to keep her from meeting this man. One night the man she was intended to marry passed by the tower. Because he was so poor he had nowhere to sleep, and the rags he wore didn't keep him warm. He crawled into the skeleton of an ox to keep warm. While he slept a giant bird came along and picked up the carcass of the animal and carried it to the top of the tower in order to eat it.

When the young man awoke he couldn't imagine how he'd gotten to the rooftop. There he met the princess, who was also surprised. She had her servants bathe him and dress him in clean clothes. She was even more surprised to discover that he was wonderfully handsome, intelligent, and learned. They fell in love quickly and she asked him to marry her. They wrote a marriage contract and let God and His angels be their witnesses to the wedding. When King Solomon found out about the wedding he knew at once that the young man and his daughter belonged together. "Blessed be the Lord Who chooses a wife for every man!" he exclaimed.

Most parents, however, didn't want to leave the matchmaking to heaven, so they hired a shadhan, a matchmaker. He or she would try to pair young people according to families. The girl always married better than her circumstances, never the other way around. It was considered unlucky to marry opposites, such as a very tall man with a very short woman, or an extremely wealthy woman with a very poor man.

The unromantic arrangement of making a match sounds as if love had no place in a marriage, but this wasn't so. Love would come, but after the wedding. God made marriage at the time of Creation not only to have children but also for companionship. "And the Lord God said: 'It is not good that man should be alone.'" (Genesis 2.18)

In Biblical times, the father of the groom paid the father of the bride a dowry for the privilege of his daughter. This was because the bride would leave her father's house and go to live with her husband's family. Her father would lose a worker and the groom would gain one.

There were times when young men married later, because they didn't have enough money for a bride.

The solution to this problem was the ketubah, a marriage contract between a husband and wife. The ketubah was a woman's protection. The groom's family did not have to provide a dowry anymore, but he promised, in writing, to pay her whatever was agreed upon by the families if he divorced her or died. This made marriage easier and divorce harder.

A ketubah, which is still used, is written by hand and often decorated beautifully, perhaps to suggest that the shared life of the bride and groom should be full of beauty. The contract is business-like, carefully spelling out what each person is to bring to the marriage, but the ketubah also promises something unwritten. It is a covenant between two people who promise to be partners in life and care for one another. The first ketubah, written by Moses at Mount Sinai, was between the Jewish people and God.

In ancient Israel, once the families agreed upon the ketubah, everyone would go to the house of the bride's parents to celebrate the kiddushin, or betrothal. The groom gave the bride something, usually a ring, in the presence of two witnesses. During the kiddushin, a period that lasted up to a year, the couple was technically married but the bride remained at home. She spent the betrothal time preparing her clothes for the actual wedding, called a nissuin, which was marked by going to the groom's house. By the Middle Ages, the two ceremonies, kiddushin and nissuin, were combined into the one ceremony that is done today.

Friday was a popular wedding day, because if the

This 19th Century ketubah from Persia
looks like an Oriental carpet.

A modern decorative ketubah.
Artist: Jonathan Kremer.
STEPHANIE SABAR/GALLERY JUDAICA

wedding took place in the morning the feast could be part of the Shabbat dinner. Tuesday was also a common day for weddings, because when God was creating the world, at the end of the third day he said twice, "It is well." There are no weddings on Shabbat or major holidays; one joy must not overshadow the other. Most weddings today are on Saturday night or Sunday. In ancient times autumn and spring were wedding seasons. In the fall the farmer's work was finished and in spring it hadn't yet begun. Wedding feasts included the whole village and lasted seven days, with lots of singing, dancing, food, and games.

All the bride's friends and relatives helped her get ready for her wedding. They washed, perfumed, and adorned the bride with jewelry, and helped her into her white gown. Then they carried her in a special chair to the groom's house. The groom wore either a brightly colored or a simple white robe. Both the bride and groom wore crowns of olive and myrtle leaves, because on their wedding day every bride and groom was queen and king. The ceremony took place under the open sky, so that they would have as many children as stars in the sky. The Songs of Songs, a love poem from the Bible, was sung, and six marriage blessings were read.

Brides and grooms no longer wear crowns and the bride is no longer carried to the groom's house, but the past still enriches the wedding ceremony. The wedding is a balance between old customs and the uniqueness every bride and groom brings to the ceremony. Rites of passage may be ancient, but they're always new for the participants.

The Shabbat before the wedding is special. The bride

and groom go to the synagogue on that Shabbat and are honored with an aliyah. After the blessings, the congregation throws candies at the about-to-be-married couple to wish them a sweet life. The bride and groom might be nervous wrecks right before the wedding worrying about wedding details. This special aliyah, called a oyf-rufn, is a playful break from wedding problems.

When two people are about to be married, it's as though they are beginning a new life. Whatever they have done in the past almost doesn't matter; they are starting fresh. The wedding day is like Yom Kippur, the Day of Atonement. A person fasts on Yom Kippur to start the year with a clean slate, and some brides and grooms fast on the day of their wedding.

Oyfrufn (ufruf in Hebrew) before wedding. Groom says blessings over Torah while friends hold tallit over his head.

BILL ARON/ART RESOURCE

Shortly before the wedding ceremony, the bride and groom are in separate rooms. The groom and his attendants are busy with the ketubah. The rabbi asks the groom if he agrees to his obligations as spelled out in the ketubah. At least two people must witness his reply. The witnesses, not the bride and groom, sign the ketubah. The bride, meanwhile, is with her attendants. When she is ready, she sits in a special chair, almost throne-like, and the groom comes to her. He takes a long look at her before she puts on her veil. Called bedeken, this custom began in Biblical times, when the groom often didn't know his bride very well. This is his assurance he's getting the woman he contracted for. It can be a last minute look at one another to be sure the marriage is what they want. If they both see what they want in the other, the bedeken becomes like an unwritten ketubah.

The groom's parents escort him and the bride's parents escort her to the huppah, the wedding canopy. The huppah came to replace the groom's house in the Middle Ages. Originally, it was made of four poles, cut from two trees planted when the bride and groom were born. The top was a tallit, and the huppah would be held by four people close to the bride and groom. Some people still use this simple huppah; others prefer an elaborate huppah made of flowers.

If a tallit is used for the canopy, it may be one the bride gives her groom. Even if he were given one for his Bar Mitzvah, the chances are he would have outgrown it and would be ready for a full-size tallit. The tallit is a special wedding gift because it has four fringes. Each of the four fringes has eight threads and thirty-two is the numerical equivalent of the Hebrew word for heart.

Bride and groom under a huppah.

Some people follow the custom of having the bride circling the groom several times, usually seven. This encircles or encloses the man and woman as they will be in their marriage. Circling may have begun as a superstition to protect the bride and groom in the belief that if they stayed in the circle, the evil spirits would not cross the line. Certain Native American tribes also have the bride circle the groom seven times.

When the bride and groom are both under the huppah, the rabbi takes a cup of wine and says the blessing over wine and then he says the betrothal blessing:

"You abound in blessings, Lord our God, Who has made us holy through Your commandments and has commanded us concerning marriages that are forbidden and those that are permitted when carried out under the canopy and with the sacred wedding ceremonies. You abound in blessings, Lord our God, Who makes Your people Israel holy through this rite of the canopy and the sacred bond of marriage."

Then the groom puts an unbroken gold ring (without gems) on the bride's index finger and says to her, "Behold, you are consecrated to me with this ring according to the law of Moses and Israel." The unbroken ring is used because it was easy to evaluate in ancient times and its wholeness symbolized the wholeness of two people coming together. It is important that the ring belong to the groom and not be lent to him.

This is the most important part of the ceremony. In ancient times, all you needed to get married was to give a woman an object worth more than a dime, have her accept it, say those words to her in front of two witnesses, and you would be married. Any time two people do these things they are married. There is no need for a rabbi. Children are taught never to pretend getting married by performing this ceremony, because if they are of Bar Mitzvah age they will be married! If the bride gives the groom a ring, she performs the same binding ceremony.

The rabbi reads the ketubah and gives it to the bride, who is responsible for its safekeeping. Seven blessings are then said by either friends or the rabbi. The blessings thank God for:

creating the fruit of the vine;
creating the universe;
creating human beings;
creating human beings in God's image in such
    fashion that they in turn can create life;
God's grace;
causing the bridegroom and the bride to rejoice;
and for creating joy and gladness, groom and bride,
    laughter, song, dancing and jubilation, love and
    harmony, peace and fellowship.

The bride and groom drink wine from the same cup after the blessing to show that they have begun their life together.

At the end of the ceremony, the groom steps on a glass which is wrapped in a napkin. This is a reminder of the destruction of the Temple. It also is a wish for as many happy years together as there are pieces of glass. It also has superstitious roots. Marriage is holy and a wedding is a wonderful event, but like all of life's passages, it is a change, and changes hold danger as well as joy. Break-

A modern wedding cup. The words on the cup say, "I am my beloved's." Th
case next to it encloses the glass that the groom steps on during the ceremon
STEPHANIE SABAR

ing the glass creates a loud noise and will scare away
anything that might disturb the passage. It also provides
a dramatic end to the ceremony. Everyone says "Mazel
Tov" when they hear the crunch, and then the bride and
groom kiss.

Right after the ceremony, the bride and groom go off
by themselves for a short time. This is called yihud,
which means being alone together. They may break
their fast at this time. When they emerge, they are finally recognized as married.

In Eastern Europe, no celebration matched the wedding feast. It was the grandest party in a person's life,

and a celebration not only of two people but two families becoming part of a larger family. The parents of the bride and groom felt that they had completed an important task when they had married off their children.

The feast was as large as a family could afford and it provided entertainment, the only rite of passage that included music. A klezmer band was hired to play music that ranged from very lively polkas to nostalgic waltzes. A badhen, a professional jester, was also part of the merrymaking. His job was to keep everyone laughing—and crying. As soon as he made them laugh he would go to the bride and say something like, "Why do you laugh? You are leaving your mama and papa and you will work every minute of your life!" The bride would look at her parents and begin to weep. The badhen would interrupt her and say, "Why do you cry? Look at your handsome brilliant husband. The way he looks would make any girl smile!" Then the poor girl, very confused by now, would look shyly at her groom, and laugh. The celebration would go on until the early hours of the morning.

Weddings are still very special, with music, dancing, and lots of food. In Israel, when a couple from a kibbutz marries, everyone on the kibbutz is invited because the entire community rejoices. Instead of a badhen, they use modern technology for tears and laughter. They run two projectors, each one showing slides of the bride and groom as they grow up. Just as the badhen would tell stories of the boy and girl growing up, the slides bring everyone up-to-date on the new couple.

When a couple marries, they do so in the hope that they will be married for the rest of their lives. In ancient times, this was almost always what happened, and only in extreme cases of unhappiness did a marriage end in divorce. The Torah permits divorce. It recognizes that not all marriages are successful. Marriage depends upon warmth and love, and if a marriage no longer gives this to husband and wife, the law provides a way out. No one can perform mitzvot with the right intention if he or she is full of anger and pain.

Once a couple decides to divorce, they first must go to civil courts to settle their separation. Then they go to a rabbi and ask him to give them a bill of divorcement, called a get. This is such a serious and sad rite that the rabbi fasts on the day of the meeting. The Talmud says that "the altar of God sheds tears" when a marriage is dissolved.

Besides the rabbi, there is also a sofer, or scribe, and two witnesses. The rabbi asks the man and woman, separately, if there is a chance of their calling the divorce off. If they both say no, which they usually do, each of them goes off to a separate room to wait for the get to be written by the sofer. This can take at least two hours, and for many people it is a painful but helpful time to mourn their marriage.

When the sofer is finished writing the get, the rabbi calls the husband and wife into the room. He asks the wife if she accepts the divorce. When she answers affirmatively, the husband says that he releases his wife from marriage and she can marry someone else. The rabbi and witnesses sign the paper. Then the husband hands the get to his wife. She puts her arms in front of her with her palms together, and he places it in her hands. Then she closes her hands around it, puts it under her arm, and walks out of the room. They are now divorced. She

From the film *Hester Street*. The rabbi is
explaining the divorce proceedings to the wife.

MIDWEST FILM PRODUCTIONS INC.

then returns and the witnesses tell the rabbi that it is the
document they signed. The sofer confirms that it is the
document he wrote. The husband says that he asked the
scribe to write it. This is all to be sure that with something as serious as divorce there are no mistakes or de-

ceptions. When the rabbi is satisfied that everything is correct, he folds the get and cuts the corners off to keep it from being used again. The ceremony is over.

A civil divorce ends a marriage with no concern for the feelings of the people involved. When a couple decides to divorce, they may stop talking to one another. Their lawyers take care of all their communication. This avoids arguments and pain, but it also takes the divorce away from the people involved. Sometimes they feel that the lawyers are fighting too hard against the person they once loved and shared a life with. The lawyers speak for the man and woman, and certain words and feelings don't get heard between them.

A get, on the other hand, is more than a legal document. Like all rites of passage, it encourages the expression of feelings. While a divorce is often a time of loss and grief, the get helps people to let go. They can abandon, without shame, their anger, promises, and expectations directed at their partner.

By permitting divorce, Jewish tradition acknowledges the courage it takes to say goodbye. It also frees the two people to start a new loving relationship with someone else. If they have children, it may help them to remember that although they have ended their claim on one another, they still have a lifelong partnership as parents. A Jewish divorce may not make the parting less sad, but it does offer a way to mourn the dead marriage and to end it by ceremony.

5

REMEMBERING

Naked I came from my mother's womb,
And naked shall I return there.
The Lord gave and the Lord took away;
Blessed be the name of the Lord.

JOB 1:21

Death is difficult to think about because no one knows what it's like to die. Its mystery makes it an often avoided but not forgotten subject. Yet dying is part of living, and thinking about it long before it happens may help to take away some of the fear and discomfort people feel when they talk about death.

It's natural to be curious about what happens after dying. Jewish tradition offers no clear picture of life after death, because the rabbis couldn't explain what they had never seen. They did, however, try to imagine it. They thought that the soul leaves the body at death and returns to God—that death is a returning to where one began. This journey is like the seasons—spring returns each year after winter. In the same way, the soul becomes part of a person when he is in the womb, and returns after the life has ended. The cycle continues when the soul returns to a new person again.

When someone close to you dies, you may feel as though part of you had died, too. Anger rises and you wonder how life can be so cruel. At this time of rage and grief, laws of mourning help to hold you together and not be crushed by feelings. From the moment someone dies, until there are no people left to remember, Jewish tradition has customs to keep memory alive and laws to cope with grief. As with all rites, death affects not only the individual but the community, too. If it's possible, people will stay with a dying person until the moment of death, and the community will support the mourners by their presence.

When a person feels he is about to die he recites the Sh'ma: "Hear O Israel, the Lord our God the Lord is One." The Sh'ma, the most important Jewish prayer, is the first prayer a child learns. Said upon awakening and going to sleep everyday, it seems right that it should be a person's last words.

As soon as the death occurs, members of the family close the eyes of the deceased and cover the face with a sheet. They also light a candle in the room and cover all the mirrors in the house. The mirrors are covered out of respect for the dead. If you look in the mirror, you see your own health and vigor reflected, and it mocks the person who no longer has a reflection and has begun to decay. The rabbis also said that this is no time to be concerned about whether your hair looks all right or if your shirt goes with your pants.

If the person who died was either a mother, father, son, daughter, brother, sister, or spouse, you are among the chief mourners, the aveilim. These mourners tear a small cut in a garment near the heart. An old vest, tie, or sweater is often used. This ancient act of tearing is called keriah. The cut is made while standing to show that despite your grief you are strong. The cut may be a safe form of self destruction. When you are wildly angry or hurt, you may feel an urge to break something, maybe even hurt yourself. Keriah offers the chance to tear, to mar something in a moment of grief. It is a release from the pain the death has caused. Keriah also expresses the tear in the relationship; the relationship has been cut off by death. The tearing can also take place at the funeral. Some people prefer not to tear their clothes but to wear a black button with a torn ribbon on it over their hearts.

The funeral is usually within twenty-four hours after the death. It is postponed only to allow a close relative from out of town time to get there. The speed of the funeral forces the family to face the death immediately and protects the dignity of the dead person by a quick burial. Being dead and unburied is considered humiliating. If the funeral is not held quickly, the body will have to have preservatives added to it to keep it from decaying. The Jewish way is to leave the body in its natural state and not use embalming fluids. The body is to return to the earth as it came, and with speed.

Someone stays with the body before the funeral. This may be a relative or friend. Whoever stays with the body will recite psalms such as the 23rd Psalm (see appendix). Until the body is buried, the family does not have to say daily prayers. Tradition recognizes this time for the mourners to be as though they were neither alive nor dead, because they hang between the two worlds. This is no time for prayer. To be obligated to sing God's praises when grieving is cruel.

The Chevrah Kadishah, the holy society, prepares the body for burial. The body is washed gently, just as it was washed at its birth. Prayers and psalms are said during the preparation. The body is dressed either in simple clothes or in a plain white robe with no pockets. This shows that this person's value was not in what was in those pockets but in the person's spirit. The person's tallit is also buried with him, with one fringe cut off. In ancient times they buried people in their everyday clothes to be sure they'd be recognized in the other world.

Just as the period before the burial is conducted with speed and simplicity, the funeral itself follows this pattern. The coffin is wood, usually pine, to allow for faster decomposition than a metal casket. In Israel the body is simply wrapped in a white shroud and buried on a bed of reeds. The simplicity not only honors the dead but also eases the burden of an expensive funeral. When the rabbis saw that people competed with one another to show how much they cared for the deceased by how much they spent on the funeral, they strongly discouraged it by forbidding metal caskets.

Before the burial, friends and relatives attend a brief service to recite the El Malay Rahamim, a special mourning prayer, and to say a few words about the person who has died. Listening to a friend, child, or spouse speak about the happy times they had and what they'll

A Jew may be buried in the tallit he wore during his life.

A funeral service in a chapel before the burial.

miss is sad, but it also offers assurance that death doesn't take everything: the memory of a face or the sound of someone's laugh outlives the death. Every person who has been important—a parent, grandparent, teacher, brother or sister—is part of others and will continue to live as long as they do.

Just as they hold the huppah at a wedding, friends and family carry the coffin to the burial site. This is a great mitzvah because it's the one act you do knowing that you can never be repaid by the person for whom you performed a kindness. While the coffin is carried, it stops seven times on its way to the grave. Sometimes the grave is circled seven times, which is like the bride circling the groom.

At the graveside, the mourners recite the Kaddish (see appendix), the traditional prayer of mourning that is recited daily for a year and on the anniversary of the death. The immediate family throws a few shovelfuls of earth on the coffin, after it has been lowered into the ground. This is often an emotional moment. The thud of the soil hitting the wooden box is a potent reminder that death is final, that you will never see this person again, and that you will have to go on living without him or her.

After the funeral, the mourners return home where friends and family serve them a meal called Seudat Havra-ah, the meal of consolation. The first food they eat is a hard-boiled egg, which is a symbol of life. This is to pull the mourners away from the cemetery and back to life.

The mourners light a candle which will burn for seven days. Candles always are part of special events such as Shabbat, holidays, Brits, and weddings. During Shivah, the seven days following the funeral, the candle is lit not in celebration but in remembrance of a human being. The wick is the body and the flame the soul or spirit. The soul, like a flame, brings light into darkness.

It is a sacred obligation to comfort mourners, whether you're close to them or only a passing acquaintance.

Helping to ease the loneliness of the mourner is a way to imitate God, because God visited Isaac when his father, Abraham, died. It is also a double mitzvah, because it's an act of kindness for the living and the dead.

Shivah, called the "days of bitterness" in the Talmud, is a time of intense mourning. The mourners, who wear dark clothes displaying keriah, attend no social events and rarely leave the house where they are observing Shivah. The community comes to them. The synagogue arranges a minyan, which is a group of at least ten people who say Kaddish, to go to the house each evening. During this period the mourners "sit" Shivah at the house of the deceased. The expression came from the old custom of sitting on the ground during mourning to show that the mourners felt diminished by the death of someone they loved. Orthodox Jews follow this custom by sitting on low stools.

Shivah is a time for the mourners to express their sorrow, cry aloud if they wish, and know that they are among people who care about them. Shivah is not a party or a way to distract the mourners from their grief by having them entertain people for seven days. The visitors bring food to the mourners to free them from cooking during this time.

When visitors enter the house, they don't come over and say hello to the mourners, as they would at a social event. The best thing to do is to go up to a mourner, say nothing, but sit beside him or her and share the silence. When the mourner feels like talking, that's when to talk. The mourner decides what to talk about, and the visitor follows the conversation. Because most people don't like being around people who are grieving, they may try to ease the grief by telling the mourner something funny. Talking about the dead person and the good times that you remember is better. The mourner may cry a little, but tears help heal. It's not necessary to say much, since just being there says something. You don't say goodbye when you leave because farewells are painful for the mourner.

Because the mourners must gradually return to life, there are limits to how long and how deeply the mourners may grieve. After Shivah, they return to work and enter the mourning period of Sheloshim. This thirty-day period is a time of reentry back into the normal world of the living, but the mourners do not yet attend parties or other celebrations.

After Sheloshim, a mourner for a father or mother continues to say Kaddish daily for eleven months following the funeral. The Kaddish is traditionally said by the children of the deceased. This is one of the most important ways to honor a parent. If a child is under thirteen, however, and he has older brothers and sisters, he doesn't have to say it. Although the Kaddish is known as the mourner's prayer and is part of the daily service, it says nothing about death. The reason it is said during mourning is that it is a prayer of trust. It affirms that there is justice in the world and meaning to life. Slowly the mourner returns to this point of view.

There are ceremonies and prayers after this period of mourning. One year after the funeral, a tombstone is set on the grave. Known as the unveiling, this is a brief ceremony attended by members of the family. Every year on the anniversary of the death, family members light a yahrzeit (memorial) candle which burns for

Placing a tombstone at the head of a grave is a
sign of respect and a way to remember the dead.

twenty-four hours. The candle is lit and Kaddish is said.
The dead are also remembered at four memorial services
during the year, at Yom Kippur, Shemini Atzeret, the
eighth day of Passover, and the second day of Shavuot.

Decorative modern yahrzeit (memorial) candle.
HEBREW UNION COLLEGE SKIRBALL MUSEUM

Having someone close to you die feels like the most important event in the world, because your world has been shattered. You may welcome the chance to grieve during Shivah. But if the death occurs during a major holiday, such as Sukkot which is a time of joy, you may not sit Shivah. You must celebrate the holiday, because although the dead person is important to you, God, the source of energy and light, is more important.

There is a custom first mentioned in the Bible of writing an ethical will. A will is the last letter a person writes and it tells the survivors what things the person is leaving to them. Anything from money to a pet parrot may be left to friends and relatives.

An ethical will is different because it doesn't promise anything material. Instead it offers the wisdom gained from having lived, and that is what it wills to relatives. Usually parents will write the ethical will or letter to their children when they are in fine health and in a moment of reflection. The will may tell how much the parents enjoyed being with their children and how they hope the children will grow to be caring sensitive people.

There is often a wish that the children will keep their link to the Jewish people and teach it to their children, too. This will be a way for the parent to feel that what they taught their children will live on. Sholom Aleichem was a Yiddish writer of short stories, many of which were very funny. His ethical will told his children that he wanted them to be good people and remain Jews, but he included something else. He asked that once a year, on the anniversary of his death, they do more than light a candle and say Kaddish. He asked them to get together and either read his ethical will or choose one of his stories, preferably a funny one, and read it aloud. He wanted to be remembered not with tears but with laughter. Writing a will long before you expect to die, even if you are a young person, gives you the chance to think about how you would like to be remembered.

AFTERWORD

When Jewish families were large and close, children were familiar with rites of passage. Children were near when a baby brother or cousin had his Brit. An older sister might marry; grandparents died. But today families are smaller and more spread apart. People live longer, and a child may rarely attend a life-cycle ceremony.

The rites described in this book give a picture of how the Jewish tradition sees human life. Living is holy—sharing your life with someone you love is a way to feel God's presence, having children is a way to be in partnership with God, and knowing about death is a reminder of your return to the Creator.

People have begun to feel that something is missing in their lives, something that punctuates the important moments, so they've revived these celebrations. Some have made up some new ones. Leaving-home ceremonies for children when they go away to college is an example. Until modern times children did not leave home until they married. Leaving home is a wonderful yet difficult event, and a ceremony that expresses these feelings is welcome. The ceremony may include a Havdalah service, which is the farewell service for Shabbat. Havdalah means separation, and this may be the first major separation of a child from his or her parents. The parents and younger brothers and sisters say a few words, and so does the person who is leaving.

Other new ceremonies celebrate women's life experiences such as menstruation, childbirth, and menopause. Some people feel that a Bar/Bat Mitzvah at thirteen happens too early in life to appreciate it. As adults they would like to reaffirm their growth in the tradition. So they have a Bar/Bat Mitzvah at thirteen year intervals such as 26, 39, and 52. Other adults who never had a ceremony at thirteen choose to study and read from the Torah as adults.

All these ceremonies, old and new, give meaning to the life cycle, offer continuity to generations past and future, and link the participant to the Jewish people.

Appendix
Glossary
Index

Appendix

Jewish prayers are always said in Hebrew. Some synagogues will also say them in English.

Shehecheyanu

> You abound in blessings, Lord our God, Ruler of the universe, Who has granted us life and sustained us and brought us to this moment.

Before Putting on Tallit

> You abound in blessings, Lord our God, ruler of the universe, Who has sanctified us with His commandments and has commanded us to wrap ourselves in [a tallit with] fringes.

Sh'ma

> Hear O Israel, the Lord our God, the Lord is One.

Betrothal Blessing

You abound in blessings, Lord our God, Who has made us holy through Your Commandments and has commanded us concerning marriages that are forbidden and those that are permitted when carried out under the canopy and with the sacred wedding ceremonies.

You abound in blessings, Lord our God, Who makes Your people Israel holy through this rite of the canopy and the sacred bond of marriage.

The Twenty-Third Psalm

The Lord is my shepherd; I shall not want.
>He maketh me to lie down in green pastures:
>He leadeth me beside the still waters.

He restoreth my soul;
He guideth me in straight paths for His name's sake.
>Yea, though I walk through the valley of the shadow of death,
>I will fear no evil, for Thou art with me;
>Thy rod and Thy staff, they comfort me.

Thou preparest a table before me in the presence of mine enemies;
Thou hast anointed my head with oil; my cup runneth over.
>Surely goodness and mercy shall follow me all the days of my life;
>And I will dwell in the house of the Lord forever.

Kaddish

Magnified and sanctified be the name of God throughout the world which He hath created according to His will. May He establish His kingdom during the days of your life and during the life of all the house of Israel, speedily, yea, soon; and say ye, Amen.

May His great name be blessed for ever and ever.

Exalted and honored be the name of the Holy One, blessed be He, whose glory transcends, yea, is beyond all praises, hymns and blessings that man can render unto Him; and say ye, Amen.

May there be abundant peace from heaven, and life for us and for all Israel; and say ye, Amen.

May He who establishes peace in the heavens, grant peace unto us and unto all Israel; and say ye, Amen.

GLOSSARY

ALIYAH—Being called up to the Torah to recite the prayers said before and after reading a Torah portion.

ASHKENAZIC JEWS—Jews descended from Eastern European families.

AVEILIM—The chief mourners: mother, father, son, daughter, sister, brother, and spouse.

BADHEN—A professional jester at a wedding.

BAR MITZVAH—Son of the commandment. The term for a thirteen-year-old boy to signify that he has reached the age of religious responsibility; the rite of passage that occurs when a boy becomes thirteen. The equivalent for girls is the BAT MITZVAH, which means daughter of the commandment.

BARUH HABA—Blessed be he who comes. A welcoming greeting. These are the first words said at a Brit Milah.

BEDEKEN—A ceremony before the wedding to permit the groom to lift the veil of the bride and see her face before he marries her.

BIMA—The raised platform of the synagogue where the Torah is read and services are conducted.

BRIT BAT—Covenant of the daughter. A welcoming ceremony for newborn girls.

BRIT HAYIM—Covenant of life. A welcoming ceremony for newborn girls.

BRIT MILAH—Covenant of circumcision. A welcoming ceremony for newborn boys.

CHAYA—A midwife.

CHEVRAH KADISHAH—A group of people who prepare a body for burial.

COVENANT—A promise or agreement.

DALED—Letter of the Hebrew alphabet.

DRASHA—A short speech about the meaning of some part of the Torah.

ELIJAH'S CHAIR—The chair used at a Brit Milah.

EL MALAY RAHAMIM—"Lord Who Is Full of Mercy," a mourning prayer said at a funeral.

GEHENNA—Hell.

GET—A bill of divorcement.

HAFTORAH—A part of the Prophets that is read after the Torah portion.

HALLAH—A braided egg bread that is eaten on festive occasions.

HAVDALAH—The ceremony that marks the end of Shabbat.

HUPPAH—The wedding canopy.

ISRAELITES—One of the three families to which Jews belong; the other two are the Kohenim and the Levites.

KADDISH—A mourning prayer that is recited for a year after a death and on the anniversary of a death.

KERIAH—The act of tearing one's garment if one is a mourner.

KETUBAH—The written marriage contract.

KIDDUSH—The Hebrew word for sanctification. A blessing said over wine to sanctify a special event such as a holiday or rite of passage.

KIDDUSHIN—Part of the wedding ceremony. It is from the Hebrew word kadosh, which means holy.

KIPPAH—A head covering worn when praying or studying.

KISEH SHEL ELIAHU—The Hebrew term for the chair of Elijah used at the Brit Milah.

KLEZMER BAND—Musicians in Eastern Europe who played music at weddings.

KOHEN—One of the three families to which Jews belong; the other two are the Israelites and the Levites.

KOHENIM—Plural of Kohen.

KVATTERIN—The godmother at a Brit Milah; she carries the baby to the mohel.

LEVITES—One of the three families to which Jews belong; the other two are the Israelites and the Kohenim.

LILITH—Adam's first wife, who supposedly took newborn children from their parents.

MAZEL TOV—Literally, "May the constellations be with you!" A form of congratulations, but most appropriate when said at a birth.

MENSCH—Yiddish for a human being with good character.

MINYAN—Ten people required when reading the Torah or saying the mourner's kaddish.

MI SHEBERAH—A blessing said before an aliyah for a person who is ill or who has been through an ordeal. The father says this blessing for his wife and baby within a month of the birth.

MITZVAH (mitzvot, pl.)—A good deed; a rule or commandment that Jews believe was given to them by God for leading a good life.

MOHEL—The person who circumcises a boy at a Brit Milah.

NISSUIN—Part of the wedding ceremony; in ancient times it was marked by the bride going to the groom's house.

ONANIM—The mourners before a funeral.

OYFRUFN—Yiddish for the special aliyah given to a bride and groom on the Shabbat before their wedding.

PIDYON HABEN—Redemption of the firstborn. The ceremony for the firstborn male child one month after his birth.

ROSH HODESH—Head of the month; the holiday that celebrates the new moon each month.

SABBATH—The seventh day of the week, a day of rest and play.

SANDEK—The person who holds the baby during the Brit Milah.

SEPHARDIC JEWS—Jews from Spain and the Middle East.

SEUDAT HAVRA-AH—The meal of consolation eaten by mourners after a funeral.

SEUDAT MITZVAH—A meal of celebration following a joyful ceremony.

SHABBAT—Hebrew for Sabbath.

SHADHAN—A professional matchmaker.

SHALOM NEKEVAH—Greeting the female. A celebration for baby girls on the first Friday night after they are born.

SHALOM ZACHAR—Greeting the male. A celebration for baby boys on the first Friday night after they are born.

SHAVUOT—A spring holiday that celebrates God giving Moses the Torah; a Yizkor (memorial) service is said in the morning.

SHEHECHEYANU—A prayer of Thanksgiving.

SHELOSHIM—A thirty-day mourning period.

SHEMINI ATZERET—The seventh day of Sukkot; a Yizkor (memorial) service is said in the morning.

SHIN—A Hebrew letter associated with tefillin.

SHIVAH—A seven-day period of mourning; the mourners stay at the house of the deceased and are visited by friends and family.

SH'MA—The most important Jewish prayer.

SIMHA—A joyous event.

SIMHAT HABAT—A birth ceremony that welcomes a baby girl as one of the Jewish people.

SOFER—A scribe who copies important documents such as a get and ketubah, as well as the Torah.

TALLIT—Prayer shawl.

TALMUD—Commentaries on the Torah.

TEFILLIN—Two boxes with prayers contained in them, and leather straps; they are worn at prayer except on Shabbat.

TORAH—The five books of Moses; also, teachings.

WIMPEL—A Torah binder made of cloth to keep the spools of the Torah together. It is often made from the diaper a baby wore at his Brit Milah, and given to a synagogue when he is a year old, or at his Bar Mitzvah.

YAHRZEIT—The anniversary of a death.

YIHUD—A short moment of privacy after the wedding ceremony before the bride and groom greet guests.

YUD—A Hebrew letter associated with tefillin.

iNDEX

93